Ultimate Guide to Expert Cruise Tips for Beginners

Wyatt J. Griffin

Life's rhythm is a blend of highs and lows; dance to its beat with grace and resilience.

Ensure your training gear is appropriate; the right shoes and attire can prevent injuries and improve performance.

Stay open-minded; even if you disagree with a book's premise, there's value in understanding different viewpoints.

Nurture mutual trust; it's the bedrock of a lasting bond.

Introduction

Welcome aboard to the ultimate guide to saving time, money, and hassle on your cruise! Whether you're a seasoned cruiser or embarking on your maiden voyage, this comprehensive guide will equip you with invaluable tips and tricks to make the most of your cruise experience.

Before you even set sail, we'll delve into the art of booking a cruise, revealing savvy hacks to secure the best deals and score significant discounts. From booking early to exploring "shoulder seasons," you'll discover how to optimize your cruise booking process.

Once you're set to sail, packing becomes an art form. Learn to pack in sets, roll your clothes efficiently, and use dryer sheets for freshness. We'll even introduce you to virtual reading materials to ensure your entertainment needs are well taken care of.

As you embark on your cruise adventure, we'll guide you through cabin hacks that transform your stateroom into a home away from home. From organization tips to ensuring a restful night's sleep, you'll discover the secrets to enhancing your cabin experience.

Traveling with young kids? We've got you covered! Child-proof your cabin with simple tape tricks and equip your little ones with a watch to keep track of their whereabouts.

When it comes to exploring ports, we've got insider tips to maximize your experience while saving money. From booking excursions in advance to negotiating with vendors, you'll be a savvy traveler at every port of call.

Hungry for savings? Discover how to dine on board like a pro with our dining hacks. Get the best tables, indulge in sweet treats, and take advantage of room service for a delightful culinary experience.

Maintaining your health and well-being on board is essential, and we've got practical tips to ensure a smooth and enjoyable journey. From staying hydrated to preventing seasickness, you'll be equipped to handle any health challenge that comes your way.

Throughout your cruise, we'll empower you with practical hacks to navigate the ship, make the most of amenities, and stay connected with fellow travelers. The cruise experience should be stress-free, and with our expert advice, you'll be well-prepared for every aspect of your journey.

So, whether you're sailing the high seas for relaxation, adventure, or both, this guide will be your trusty companion. Set sail with confidence, knowing that you're armed with the ultimate guide to saving time, money, and hassle on your cruise. Get ready for an unforgettable voyage, filled with cherished memories, newfound friends, and a dash of magic on the high seas. Bon voyage!

Contents

CHAPTER 1

BOOKING A CRUISE HACKS

Follow these tips when booking your next cruise. You'll rest assured that you got the best deal possible. Cruise booking is tricky. We have you covered!

BOOK EARLY TO SAVE

Typically, booking far in advance (a year plus) or very close to your departure date will offer the best price. **Cruise lines want you to book early**. The sooner they're able to fill cabins, the better off they are in terms of forecasting. As such, they'll incentivize you with lower prices on cruises in the distant future.

When booking in advance, assure that your cancellation policy allows for a full refund (with deposit). This is very important! Then use a Price Alert to monitor fare changes (see next tip).

SET A PRICE ALERT

This is one of biggest opportunities to **save hundreds**, and sometimes thousands, of dollars.

After booking early, employ a **Cruise Fare Monitor**. Most of these services cost money. But, here we'll provide two that are completely free to use.

Ship Mate Mobile App: This is a free mobile app to prepare for your upcoming sailing. In addition to a bunch of fun features, the app provides a free cruise fare monitor. Simply save your cruise to your "My cruises" section of the app. Then, in that saved cruise, tap "Price Alert." You'll have the option to set that alert by cabin type (inside, ocean-view, balcony, or suite). Using these links, you can download Ship Mate for iOS and Ship Mate for Android for free!

Cruiseline.com: This is a web-based tool also offering free price-drop alerts. It works the same as with Ship Mate. You can find instructions on setting that alert here.

Once set on either platform, you'll get an email with any price change over 1%. If you're within your allowed cancellation period, you can immediately take advantage of this. Typically your agent will provide either **on-board credit or a free upgrade** to your cabin category. We've had readers save thousands of dollars!

BOOK ALASKA EXTRA EARLY (STARBOARD CABIN)

Cruising to Alaska, book (**starboard side cabin**) early!

Alaska has a short season and limited sailings. Balcony cabins for those sailings tend to sell out much quicker than a typical sailing. Particularly, balcony cabins on the Starboard side of the ship.

You'll be heading North, so will want that starboard (right-hand-side) **view of the coast!** To assure this, you'll need to book over a year in advance. We recommend **at least 16 months before you sail**.

BOOK LAST MINUTE

This works particularly well for those with flexibility and a sense of adventure. Specifically, retirees, students, teachers, and others with long periods of flexibility. The more flexible you are with cruise line, itinerary length, and destination, the more options you'll have for cheap cruises.

The likelihood of taking advantage of **last-minute cruises** is even greater if you live by a port city.

Why does this work?

Cruise ships have an average capacity of 100%. They would rather sell the cabin for $25 per night than to have it go vacant. And, we often see cruises for that cheap!

USE A FARE MONITORING TOOL

We have the best software tool available for **finding last minute cruise deals**. With this free fare-monitoring tool, you'll never miss another great cruise deal.

Cruise Deals App: this free mobile app allows you to **declare your own price**. You'll get a notification immediately when a cruise becomes available that fits your stated criteria. Once downloaded, you choose your preferred departure port. In that port section, you can **set an alert** based on price per night. For example, you could set it up to receive a notification any time a cruise leaving Boston drops below $40 per night.

You can download <u>**Cruise Deals App for FREE here**</u>.

BEST TIMES TO BOOK

Cruise lines will periodically host deals throughout the year. These sales are generally unpredictable, but there are **two specific times** of year which can be expected.

Black Friday & Cyber Monday: During the few days after Thanksgiving, cruise lines consistently offer the best deals of the year. This ranges from "buy one get one free" to thousands in on-board credit. The deals tend to start the day after Thanksgiving and last for a few days.

Wave Season: Nope, this is the time of year when waves are huge so cruises are cheap :-) Rather, it refers to a wave of cruise bookings that flood the industry in the first quarter of every year. While this period doesn't have a defined range, it is conventionally thought to start in early January and last through the first quarter of the year. The deals offered during this period aren't quite as good as Black Friday and Cyber Monday, but are better than the rest of the year on average.

USE A CRUISE AGENT… YES, SERIOUSLY

As a society, we've been conditioned to book directly with the source. Airfare, hotel, rental cars… all have become a commodity. Most people no longer rely on travel agents for any of these travel needs. While we wouldn't consider an agent as "essential" when booking a hotel, this is **NOT the case with cruises**.

It's likely that the travel agent will NOT be able to get you a cheaper deal than if you were to go direct. Then why use an agency? For **two main reasons**.

1. **Industry knowledge**: A good agent will hopefully know many of the tips found in this book. Your agent will make sure that you avoid all pitfalls and make the most of your vacation.
2. **Your representation**: Dealing with the cruise line can be a pain. You don't want to be the one calling up Carnival or Royal Caribbean with issues. An agent can deal with that for you. As an example, your cruise price might drop using the tip we provided earlier. Once that happens, you'll probably need help capitalizing on this. An agent will have the know-how to capture that value.

FOR CHEAPER RATES, LOOK AT "SHOULDER SEASON"

There's "Peak Season" and "Off Season" for cruise destinations. But, some don't know that there's also a **"Shoulder Season."** It falls on the front and back ends of Peak Season. During these few weeks, cruises are less expensive, but you still benefit from the perks of this popular cruise period.

BOOK A "GUARANTEED STATEROOM"

To get the **absolute cheapest rate**, you can book what's called a "**guaranteed stateroom**." It assures you a cabin type, but your specific room assignment isn't immediately assigned.

The potential risk is that you end up in a noisy or otherwise undesirable location.

The potential upside is that you get bumped up a class of cabin.

Your only guarantee in this situation is that you get the cheapest rate!

BOOK A "GUARANTEED STATEROOM" - NEXT LEVEL

This hack takes a bit of work, but can pay off in the long run.

While booking, attempt to book a "guaranteed stateroom" for a cabin category in which there is **no available assigned options**. For instance, if you're looking at the "ocean-view cabin" category for a particular ship… if you see no assigned room options, but a "guaranteed stateroom" choice, that's promising. It could mean that there are no more staterooms available in that category. If that's the case, the cruise line would never downgrade you a class. The hope is that they instead bump you up a level.

This is a tricky game though, so be sure you're fine with that guaranteed stateroom category!

BOOK YOUR NEXT CRUISE WHILE ON-BOARD

Some of the best booking incentives are offered **while on a cruise**. These come in the form of discounts, on-board credit and reduced deposits. Often, they're also offered as "**risk free**." The cruise can be refunded or date switched around much more easily than if booked regularly.

If you're worried about not going through your agent, then don't fret. Once booked, the cruise line recognizes and **compensates the agent / agency** that booked you onto that sailing! They'll get the commission without lifting a finger.

As an added bonus - Booking a cruise while on a cruise also dulls the pain felt on that last day. You'll get off of your ship knowing that another cruise is on the horizon.

CHECK FOR FREE CRUISE INSURANCE

Some credit card companies offer **free travel insurance** if booking with that card. Before booking, check the insurance policies of your credit cards. Consider using one that offers travel benefits.

If your credit card company does not offer any benefits, you can consider Cruise Insurance. On average, you'll find it costs roughly 7% of your total cruise cruise cost for coverage. For specifics on what you can expect to pay, check out this post on Cruise Travel Insurance.

LOCATION, LOCATION, LOCATION

Your cabin location could **make or break your cruise** if you're sensitive to noise or motion sickness.

If **noise** bothers you, get a cabin at the end of the hall, where there will be less foot traffic.

If **motion sickness** is an issue, get a cruise cabin in the middle of the ship. The center of a cruise ship experiences significantly less movement when compared to its ends.

If you have **trouble walking**, get a cabin nearby the elevators.

BOOK IN BULK

Most people don't know this, but booking a group can result in a **free cruise** for the organizer.

Often cruise lines will **encourage group bookings** by giving on-board credit, upgrades and even a free cruise.

As an example, Princess offers a free sailing with 16 bookings and Crystal gives a free cruise at 10.

Get the co-workers or family together for a cruise and you could be sailing for free!

MILITARY, RESIDENTS, & EVEN TEACHER DISCOUNTS

Make sure to ask about every type of discount offered by the cruise line. You could be **eligible for savings** without even knowing it. Here are some examples of those groups offering discounts:

- Military
- AARP
- Residency Rates
- Teachers

These discounts tend to be roughly **5-10%**, which can be significant on a cruise purchase. Ask your agent to list every available discount.

BOOKING HACKS

EBATES CASH BACK

Here's a hack that few know about. You can actually get up to 10% cash back when booking a cruise by using an ecommerce platform called Ebates.

While Ebates itself doesn't sell cruises, they do link to popular sites with an attached discount code for cash back. At the time of writing this, Expedia was offering 3% cash-back while Priceline was offering 5%! On a cruise for two, at $1,500 a piece, that's total cash back of **$150 in your pocket**. In doing so, however, you lose the benefits of working with a travel agent. The cash back percentage fluctuates and we've seen it as high as 10%, so check what it is currently by clicking through if interested.

Using this Ebates link, you'll get an additional $10 added to your account.

INSURE BUT NOT THROUGH THE CRUISE LINE OR AGENCY

Some people are risk takers and others have to play it safe. If you're of the latter type, you'll want to **book cruise insurance**.

Here are some of the ways insurance can save the day.

- Medical emergencies & transportation
- Trip cancellation or disruption
- Missed travel connections
- Cruise line default

Agencies and cruise lines' policies **don't offer adequate coverage** and typically **cost more** than the alternative. You'll find cruise lines actually farm out the responsibility to a large insurance company. As such, it's more expensive (two companies are now taking a cut of the profits) and the experience communicating through the extra party is inefficient. Recently, major cruise lines were actually sued for not making it obvious that they weren't the companies insuring their customers.

You'll find the best coverage/price combo by using InsureMyTrip. The site allows you to easily compare multiple plans and providers in one place. You can also filter based on your specific insurance needs.

ENJOY THE PRE-CRUISE PERIOD

Congrats - you've booked a cruise! The **fun starts NOW** so don't wait until you've stepped foot on the ship. Anticipation is half the fun, and we have the perfect tool to make the most of your pre-cruise period.

The Ship Mate Cruise App is FREE for iOS and Android and offers all kinds of **fun ways to prepare and get excited** for your cruise, including the following:

- See who's on your ship
- Track your ship's current location
- Preview your ship's deck maps
- Chat with other cruisers
- Get helpful ship and port tips
- Book excursions
- View user photos
- Much more

Download **Ship Mate for iOS** and **Ship Mate for Android** free!

THAT'S THE TICKET

If you're waiting for a cruise ticket to show up in the mail, you'll be disappointed. **Cruise lines and agencies don't actually mail you a physical ticket**.

We were bummed the first time we realized this, because we wanted to surprise our mother with a cruise ticket inside her Mother's Day card.

Fortunately, we found a service that provides this. For a couple bucks, you can **have a custom cruise ticket generated in a few hours** and print it immediately after.

We've tried a few of these services and here's the best printable cruise ticket that we continue to use regularly.

CHAPTER 2

PACKING

A cruise isn't a "normal" type of vacation. There are a lot of nuances to this type of travel. We'll make sure you're packed most efficiently.

PACK IN SETS

You'll be taking part in a variety of activities on your cruise vacation. These will require significantly different attire for each. To make it easier to pack, **think in terms of "outfits"** rather than individual items.

You're going to need an outfit for the following:

- Dinners (semi-formal)
- Formal Dinner
- Poolside
- Active (gym, sports, daytime walking)
- Ports (depending on the itinerary, this will vary)
- Nightlife (casino, clubs, piano bars, etc)

USE A CRUISE PACKING CHECKLIST

There are many items you likely wouldn't think of when heading to your cruise, like your cabin luggage tags.

We always use a **cruise packing checklist** to assure we don't forget anything. As a free gift to you, here's our pre-populated, <u>**Printable Cruise Packing** Checklist</u>.

That will get you started with many of the essentials. It also includes space to add your own custom items!

CAP IT

When packing your suitcase on your way to the cruise or heading home (sad face), this hack comes in very handy.

Use a **shower cap** to wrap around your sneakers. It will keep the dirt and grime away from the rest of your items. If you don't have any lying around at home, ask your cabin steward for a couple.

CEASE THE CREASE

Irons aren't allowed on most ships, but you'll want to be crease-free for dinner and other activities.

One great hack to avoid creases during your travel… use **tissue paper** with those delicate items then stick them in a dry clean bag before packing those away. That will significantly limit the creasing during your travels.

DRYER SHEET FRESHNESS

Stick a **dryer sheet** or two in your packed luggage. This will keep your items fresh and smelling lovely while they make their eventual way to your cruise cabin!

GO VIRTUAL WITH YOUR READING MATERIAL

Reading on a cruise is lovely. The wind, the sun and a good book! But, trying to take multiple books with you on your travels can be a pain… literally.

Don't lug heavy books on your vacation. Instead, **download them** to a Kindle, iPad, or other tablet. You can get as many books as you want into a device the size of one short story!

An added bonus... you can read at night!

If you're really opposed to reading on a digital device, you can still avoid lugging heavy books. Instead of bringing your own, visit your **on-ship library**!

THE BEST RESOURCE FOR FREE EBOOKS

Books can be expensive and risky. At $10 per book, you don't even know what you're getting. What if we told you that you could get all of the **latest thrillers, biographies, classics** and more… for free?! And, without even leaving your living room.

You can - at **your local library**! Most people don't know, but your library has a ton of digital books (audible and ebooks) for you to choose from. And, they're FREE! The limit on our local library account is 25 books. We'll load up with a dozen or more for every cruise. If we don't like it, we'll skip to the next one.

At Barnes & Noble, that would cost hundreds of dollars. Not at your library! Visit your library's web site and get an account today. Then you can start downloading books into your smartphone immediately from the comfort of your home.

UNDIE-SHOES

Roll your underwear up and stick them **tightly within your shoes**. Not only will that save space, but will also keep your shoes nicely protected during the trip.

THREAD YOUR NECKLACE

If you're worried about your necklaces getting tangled up during travel, try this hack. Thread yours **through a straw** and fasten your necklace. That way, it'll remain fully stretched and untangled.

ORGANIZE EARRINGS

Earrings tend to get tangled and lost during travel. Here's a great hack to keep those organized and tangle free. Put a set of **earrings through the holes on a single button**. Fasten the backs on the other side of the button holes and those will be secure and organized.

RAZOR PROTECTOR

Protect both your shaving razor and your fingers with this hack.

When packing your razor, take a **binder clip and open it over the head** of your razor. Clip it directly over the head so that the entire end is covered by the clip. That will protect the blades from getting gunked up in your travel bag. It will also protect you from slicing off a finger. You'll need all 10 for the buffet!

PHOTOGRAPH YOUR LUGGAGE

Unfortunately, baggage gets lost at times. If this happens, the airport staff will ask you for a detailed description of your items. You'd be surprised at how limited your recollection is of these items when put in this position. **Take a photo of your bags** beforehand and you can refer to that in the chance that your bags get misplaced.

ROLL WITH IT

If you need some extra space in your suitcase, try **rolling your clothes**. You'll be surprised at how much space you can save rolling versus folding.

And, this limits the wrinkles you'll get in your clothing!

SHIRT COLLAR HACK

If you're trying to keep a crisp collar during your travels, try using a rolled up belt to hold that collar in place.

Lay the folded shirt down. Then take the **rolled up belt** and place it within the buttoned collar. Let it unwind to fit the collar snugly. This will make sure it doesn't get collapsed by other items in your suitcase.

NO LEAKS ON THIS SHIP

For all of your liquid items, **make sure they can't leak**. This simple hack will assure your items stay dry.

Cut out little squares of **Saran wrap** (roughly the size of a coaster). Open each liquid bottle and drape a plastic square over the top of the opening. Then return the cap and shut tightly. There's no way you'll have a leak with this hack!

PROTECT YOUR WINE

The best way to support your bottle of wine is to **use a pair of shoes**! Take each end of the bottle and slide a tennis shoe over-top, turning the shoes so they line up perfectly. That will protect the bottle from any harder items, assuring that you're not wearing red all week.

ROLL YOUR SCARVES

Roll your scarves around an **empty paper towel tube** to keep the compact and without crease.

MARK AS FRAGILE

This is a controversial hack that might offend some. If you **mark your luggage as "fragile,"** then it will be loaded on the top and offloaded first. In addition to getting treated with more care, it'll also speed up your travel.

CHAPTER 3

WHAT TO BRING

You'd never think to bring some of these recommended items. These relatively inexpensive, essentials could be the difference between a good and great cruise!

TRAVEL COFFEE MUG

The coffee mugs on the ship are a joke. They look like they belong in a doll house.

When you get up after a long night of karaoke and piano bars, you need your caffeine. And not 6 ounces at a time. Instead, bring **your own insulated coffee mug**. It will hold 4x the coffee and it will keep it hot for hours.

This is our **favorite travel coffee mug**.

BRING A NIGHT LIGHT

When getting up to use the restroom in the middle of the night, you'll want some help. You're in tight quarters, it's dark, and you don't want to wake up your cabin mate. Hitting a switch is risky… it could light up the entire cabin, or maybe just the bathroom light. Either way, it'll likely be too bright.

Avoid stubbing your toe and waking up everyone in the room, **bring a night light** to leave by your bedside. Here's our **favorite travel nightlight**. Not only is it motion-activated, but it also has a magnetic base. Since your cruise cabin walls are metal, you can stick it just about anywhere in your cruise cabin!

PLAYING CARDS & SMALL GAMES

You'll likely have a lot of down time during the week. When laying out at the pool, killing time before dinner, or when the weather isn't ideal, you'll want to entertain yourself.

A set of **Playing Cards** offers a great way to bond with your ship mates and have fun in between events.

PROBIOTIC HELP

Whenever we cruise, we tend to over-indulge on the food. It's tough not to with so many great options; and the convenience is just too tempting.

One hack we use to preempt this gluttonous stretch... **probiotics**!

We'll load up an arsenal beforehand and take daily throughout the cruise. This helps to avoid bloating and to feel much better than we otherwise would!

We use **this product from Vitamin Bounty** at least once per day between Breakfast and Lunch.

CLOTHES PINS

Take a few clothes pins with you - they'll come in super handy for a couple reasons.

You can **hang up wet clothes** on the drying line in your bathroom shower. When you get home from the pool, you won't want soggy clothes sitting around all night.

Also, you can keep your cabin extra dark by pinning **your window shades** tightly with these.

JEWELRY PILL ORGANIZER

Don't let your jewelry get all tangled up during the travels. And, don't try to lug around a huge jewelry box to keep your items safe.

Here's the hack - bring a **daily pill box** (normally for organizing your medication) to hold your earrings, necklaces, rings, and more.

They'll stay organized, safe, and inconspicuous. And, you can even organize your week's adornments.

They're less than $5 on Amazon!

EXTRA POWER

We all need the "essentials" when we cruise. Like our iPhones, iPads, laptops, mp3 players, cameras, gaming devices, hair dryers, speakers, and many other "must have" accessories. Unfortunately, cruise cabins aren't set up to accommodate our growing electrical needs.

Typically, your stateroom will have **only one outlet with two plugs** positioned in your cabin's main living area. If you're like us, this is not nearly enough to keep you juiced.

This is our solution. We always bring <u>this Cruise Power Strip</u>. Plug this device in and you'll be able to keep all of your electronic goodies powered and ready to go. **NOTE**: standard power strips are banned by most cruise lines. If they have "surge protection" or extension cords, they'll likely be confiscated. The model linked to above was made specifically to adhere to the cruise lines' policies.

Using this device, you'll also make a lot of friends at the airport. Turning one outlet into five can make you four new friends very quickly!

CONTROL YOUR WIRES

Don't let your chargers, USB cords, and earphones get into a tangled mess in the bottom of your purse or bag. Here's a hack that involves a common household item.

Use an **empty sunglass case** to hold all of these wires. You'll keep them protected from getting damaged and organized so they're not annoyingly coiled up with your stuff.

BRING A BED SHEET

When we cruise, we always bring a **cheap bed-sheet**. It takes up very little space in our suitcase and we use it at every port when heading to the beach. Or, step up your beach game even more with this <u>Travel Beach Mat</u>. It fits in the palm of your hand and unfolds to fit the entire family.

While we're laying out in comfort, others are waiting in line to rent beach chairs for $25 a piece.

THANK YOU CARDS

You can get **"thank you" cards** at the dollar store. We like to give these out to staff members at the end of the week. For a few dollars, you can make a real difference in the staff's day.

Or for a few extra dollars... we recently found and picked up these <u>Cruise Staff Thank You Cards</u> made specifically for Cruise Crew. Our last room attendant was in tears when receiving it and treated like his family for the rest of the cruise.

CRUISE CABIN ORGANIZER

There's very little shelf and closet space in your cruise cabin. Without a little extra help, your counters will be piled up with stuff. To avoid this mess, pick up an **Over the door Hanging Organizer**.

They're perfect for storing lotions, makeup, hats, shoes, electronics, and all other items that would normally cause clutter. You can hang these on the back of your cruise cabin door leading to the bathroom, closet or adjoining stateroom.

This is our favorite **Organizer on Amazon**. It's made specifically for cruising (it's flame retardant to adhere to cruise policy) and is easily packed.

WHAT TO PACK

AVOID A SLEEPLESS WEEK

Throughout your cruise, you'll have a set of strangers on your right and left-hand sides of your cabin. These people could be partiers, parents with babies, or newlyweds (mmhmm). In all cases, the extra noise could make for a rough week. Take precaution.

A **simple pair of** **$4 Earplugs from Amazon** could save your slumber and your cruise.

BREAK WIND

Cruise ships are often **incredibly windy** on the top deck. Even during warmer months, it can tend to get chilly outside as a result. Bring a windbreaker with you to avoid the heavy breeze and chills!

SPRAY OUT WRINKLES

You'll want to look your best while dining and enjoying your ship's nightlife. Make sure your pants and shirts are wrinkle free. Bring along some Downy **Wrinkle Release Spray** and give your articles a spray before hanging int he closet.

When you're ready for them, they'll look like they're straight from the cleaners.

PLENTY OF MEDS

If you're on a regular medication routine, make absolute sure to pack these and them some. We recommend taking a **couple extra days** worth just in case. You never know where you could get stranded, so it's better to be safe than sorry!

Also - make sure to keep these in your **carry-on bag** if you'll need them within six hours of boarding the ship.

BAG IT

You'll be getting very active throughout your sailing. Chances are, you won't have access to laundry facilities. To keep your soiled items separate from your clean stuff, bring a **collapsible laundry bag**. It'll keep things organized and your cabin smelling fresh. This is our favorite <u>travel laundry bag</u>.

STICKY PAD

Sticky notes can be used in a number of helpful ways on your cruise.

Leave **instructions** for your maintenance staff. Have them bring extra pillows, ice or whatever else you need. Just leave a note on your mirror.

Leave **notes** on the doors of friends and family to let them know where you'll be or where to meet you.

Place a sticky **on your own door** to easily find it amongst a sea of cabins.

BRING A PEN

A pen will come in handy throughout your cruise. It'll be particularly helpful when its time to fill out your customs forms. Typically there are **too few pens** for the number of passengers and this tends to be a bottle neck in the booking process. You'll get to the Lido Bar four minutes sooner by bringing your own pen.

CHAPTER 4

FLIGHT, HOTEL & TAXI

You want to start your cruise off on the right foot. With these travel hacks, we'll help you to avoid common problems ranging from an uncomfortable transfer to a missed flight.

FLIGHT, HOTEL & TAXI

UP TO 70% OFF HOTELS!

We're very proud to be able to offer this cruise hack. We've recently partnered with Priceline to offer up to 70% off cruise hotels.

By purchasing this ebook, you have access to these rates. We're not allowed to advertise these anywhere online and we ask that you **please do not share the link** below with others. The prices you'll find are for "Closed User Groups" only.

Click here to find your Cruise Port Hotel for up to 70% off!

Seriously... compare the rates you'll find there with those on Priceline.com, Expedia, Travelocity, or anywhere else. You should be able to save some serious money with this tip.

If you're able to take advantage of these discounted hotel rates, please email us and let us know!

FLIGHT, HOTEL & TAXI

FLIGHT PURCHASE - BEST TIME TO BUY

If you'll be flying to your departure port, follow these tips to get the **best deal on your flight**.

- The best time to buy a plane ticket is on **Tuesday at 3PM** (EST) for the cheapest fare
- Flying out **early** tends to be cheaper than later flights
- **Wednesday** is the cheapest day to fly
- Book your flight **42 days before flying**. That's the exact time found to be cheapest. If it's a holiday or other peak time to fly, don't follow this rule.

FLIGHT, HOTEL & TAXI

DELETE BROWSER COOKIES

It's assumed that flight search engines are using "cookies" to identify your purchase intent. It's possible that they're able to increase the displayed cost due to your return visits. To be assured, **clear your browser's cookies** to eliminate that extra info provided to the seller.

CHECK ON MOBILE BEFORE BOOKING

In addition to tracking "cookies," providers can also check your "IP location." If you're searching for a flight from your Beverly Hills home, you may see a different rate than someone searching from Detroit.

To disallow this extra piece of location data, you can **search for your flight on your mobile device** rather than your desktop computer. Make sure to turn off your wireless access and to use LTE or 4G. It might be worth a look before committing from your desktop.

CHOOSING SEATS WISELY

When selecting seats for two people, most people grab either the aisle and middle or window and middle.

Instead, **get the window and aisle**. That way, you're much more likely to have the entire row to yourself when nobody selects the middle.

If someone does get the middle, he will be more than willing to swap for whichever you'd prefer.

FLIGHT, HOTEL & TAXI

GUARANTEE THAT YOU MAKE YOUR CRUISE

The typical flight insurance helps you in the rare situation that you can't make your flight or have to cancel it.

One of the most common ways that a cruise vacation ends in disaster is a missed flight.

We've found a product that **ensures you'll make your cruise**. It's as if it were made specifically for cruise travelers.

It's called **Freebird**. For **$19 (each leg)**, you'll insure your flight. If it gets canceled or delayed, you'll get a notification from their mobile app immediately. They'll show you every option you have on every airline (not just the one on which you were booked). While everyone on your flight is at the airline counter trying to get out on the next flight, you'll be booked without worry. And, the best part is, you'll likely get reimbursed by the first flight provider. Often, Freebird customers walk away ahead a few hundred dollars when experiencing a canceled flight.

Consider purchasing **Freebird**… at least for the flight **to your cruise**.

FLIGHT, HOTEL & TAXI

FREE AIRPORT WIRELESS

Often you can hack your way into the wireless paid network at airports. Simply add "?.jpg" to the end of any URL. This works because airports don't block images from coming through. Adding this URL end-piece tricks the network into thinking the page is a picture. For example: www.cnn.com?.jpg.

FLIGHT, HOTEL & TAXI

DON'T USE A TAXI

Taxis will **cost significantly more** than the relatively new options of Uber and Lyft.

If you haven't yet given them a try, don't be nervous. You'll find that they're actually much less intimidating than hailing a cab.

You'll need to download the app first. Once you do, the process is very simple.

If you don't yet have an account, use these links below to get your **first ride FREE**.

Uber: <u>Free $5 in credit using this download link</u>. Click that link and download the mobile app. Open it up once downloaded and you'll get your first ride (up to $20) absolutely free.

Lyft: <u>Free $10 in credit using this download link</u>. If you already have Uber but not Lyft, you can use that link to get your first ride free (up to $10). The app is almost identical to Uber.

CONSIDER AIRBNB

Depending on your departure port, **AirBnB** might be a better option than a hotel. If you're not familiar with the service, AirBnB allows very short-term rentals of private homes and apartments. You have the option of renting the entire space, or staying with some welcoming guests.

Either way, you can use the link below to score **$40 off** of your first rental!

Click for: **$40 in Free AirBnB Credit**

Or, rent out your home while cruising. Some members of our cruise community have actually **made money while on a cruise** by renting out their place for more than their cruise cost!

FLIGHT, HOTEL & TAXI

KEEP YOUR HOTEL EXTRA DARK

Want a good night sleep? Keep your hotel room extra dark using this hack.

Grab the **pants hangers from your hotel closet** and use the clips to clamp the curtains together. This should eliminate most of the light that would otherwise sneak in.

Then, roll up a bathroom towel and put it in front of the crack in your door.

It will be so dark, you'll need to make sure to set an alarm!

FLIGHT, HOTEL & TAXI

USE YOUR AAA MEMBERSHIP

Many hotels offer a 5-10% **discount to AAA members**. This can save you enough for an extra couple drinks!

YOU CAN BRING WATER THROUGH AIRPORT SECURITY

Most people think that you can't bring water through airport security. This isn't true. You can't bring "liquids" through security over their 3 ounce limit.

You are able to bring as much water as you'd like. Here's the hack… **freeze your water**. It's then a solid and then able to get through security. Not only can you get your water through, it'll be super cold when you eventually drink it.

FLIGHT, HOTEL & TAXI

GETTING FREE WIFI

While traveling, you'll likely be using your devices and in need of wifi. When coming across a wifi network requiring a password, don't fret. You can typically **find passwords on FourSquare**. Check it out and you'll be using free wifi in no time.

DO NOT DISTURB... OR ROB

Placing your hotel room's "**Do not disturb**" sign on your door decreases chances of getting robbed.

Even if you're out on the town, others will assume you're in the room as long as that sign is up.

GET AROUND THE COOL CAP

Most hotel rooms govern the temperature in your room. You'll only be able to crank it down so low. This isn't cold enough for some. Fortunately, there's a **hack around this temperature limit**.

- On the A/C unit, hold down the "display" button
- While holding that button, press "off"
- Release off, continue to hold down display, and Press the "up" arrow button
- Release all buttons

That should **reset the cool cap** and allow for you to set your limit to cooler than normal. It's said to also eliminate the motion detection some rooms use to limit airflow.

ORDER FOOD FROM AMAZON PRIME IN YOUR ROOM

Hotel room service can be very pricey. If you're an **Amazon Prime** member, you can have restaurants **deliver to you for free**. You'll save money and get a much better meal.

If you don't yet have **Amazon Prime,** check it out here.

CHAPTER 5

CABIN HACKS

Your cruise cabin can be very uncomfortable if unprepared. You'll be spending lots of time here. Use these Cruise Cabin Hacks to make the most of your small space.

CRUISE CABIN HACKS

GET A FREE UPGRADE

When you get on the ship, you'll see a huge swarm of people at the customer service desk trying to get upgrades. This is the least likely chance you'll have to score a free bump in cabin category.

Instead, wait until **after you've disembarked your first port**. Often, there will be vacancies at this time. Some will have had to leave the cruise. Others will have been written off by the cruise lines after missing their initial departure and not being able to make it to the first port of call.

Your odds are greatly increased after Port 1 vs. Day 1!

USE CREDIT FOR AN UPGRADE

Before your sailing, it's not possible to apply your on-board credit for an upgrade. That's unfortunate, because cruise lines have been giving out a lot of credit with bookings lately!

But, most don't know… you can actually apply these credits towards a potential **upgrade once you set sail**. If you have credit and want a better room, give it a try after you set sail!

CRUISE CABIN STEREO SYSTEM

Most hotel rooms come equipped with a **radio** that you can plug into your smartphone to amplify its sound. This isn't the case with cruise cabins.

We suggest one of two options.

1. Stick your device **into one of the water cups** in your cruise cabin. Make sure the speaker side is faced down into the cup. That will amplify the sound and better project it throughout the cabin.
2. If you're looking to really start the party, get a **bluetooth speaker** to pair with your device. You can take it with you to the shuffleboard court, beach, hot tub, or wherever you'd like. This is our absolute favorite model: Bose Soundlink.

EARPLUGS COULD SAVE YOUR SANITY

You never know what kind of **cruise neighbors** you'll get. We all hope for the nice old couple that's in bed by 7pm, but that's not always the case.

If instead, you're neighbored up with some babies or honeymooners (wink, wink), then earplugs could **save your slumber**.

You could also be in a heavily trafficked hallway. People tend to have conversations as their walking through the corridors and the doors typically won't completely shield this noise. With earplugs, you won't hear a thing.

PUNCH YOUR CARD

Losing your cabin key is annoying. You'll have to wait in line at the service desk and deal with judgmental eyes as they reassign you a key.

Sometimes you'll even get fined for losing your key card.

To avoid this, **wear it around your neck**! Bring a cruise lanyard have it close by whenever you need it. You can stick credit cards and cash in there as well.

This is the best **Cruise Card Lanyard set** we've found. It comes in a bunch of fun colors and designs!

CRUISE CABIN HACKS

BONUS SECRET CHARGING STATION

On most flat-screen televisions (most cruise lines now have these), you'll find a **USB input in the back** of the device. You can use your mobile device's charging cable to hook up to this for some extra juice.

GET COMFY LIKE HEFNER

Don't pack **a robe** - it'll take up way too much space. Ask your room steward for one if you're a "robe guy / gal" and he'll be happy to provide this for you.

ELIMINATE WRINKLES

You're bound to get some **wrinkles in your clothes** while traveling. Here's a few tips to remove these so you're looking your best on "formal night."

1. Bring a **water spray bottle** and gently mist your items while hanging them in the closet. Within a few hours, you'll be wrinkle free.
2. **Steam your items** as you take a hot shower. The bathrooms are so small, that they tend to fill up quickly with steam. This will melt the creases away.
3. Bring along a small **wrinkle releaser** of your choosing. Our favorite is <u>Downy Travel Sized Bottles</u>.

HACKING THE LIGHT SWITCH

Many cruise cabins now require your room key to turn on the lights.

This can be inconvenient at times. To **"fool" the switch**, bring any old membership card (Walgreens, Costco, etc) and stick it in there.

When rushing back to your room to use the restroom after the buffet, you won't need to fumble with your card key.

CRUISE CABIN ORGANIZER

This is an essential.

Since your square footage is limited, **use vertical space** for storage and organization.

This **Over the Door Hanging Organizer** is ideal for that. It hangs over your cruise cabin door in seconds and can fit many of the items you'll have on hand, including:

- Lotions
- Hats
- Books & Magazines
- Shoes & Sandals
- Toiletries
- Hair products
- Makeup
- Documents

Your room will be much more comfortable without all of the clutter.

CRUISE CABIN HACKS

ASK FOR HANGERS

Your cruise cabin steward will be glad to provide **extra clothes hangers**.

In your cabin, you'll likely find 10 or so hangers. For two people, this won't be enough for a 7 night sailing. Rather than folding your clothes up in the bins, simply **request more** from your steward and hang up your items.

HANG IT UP

Most people don't notice the **hang-dry line** in the shower.

It pulls from one end to the other and allows for easy hanging of bathing suits, towels, or other.

This will be much more convenient than draping your soggy items throughout the cabin.

DIRTY BAG

It's likely you won't be doing laundry while on your cruise. No prob! Just toss those soiled items away in any **plastic or mesh bag** for laundry storage.

This helps keep them out of the way of your nice, clean stuff.

This one is our favorite **collapsible travel laundry bag**. It's lightweight and takes up virtually no space when empty.

BRING NOTES

Post it notes are cheap, easy to pack, and come in **very handy** on the ship.

Use them on cabin doors to let friends and family know where you'll be.

Leave them in your own cabin to let your room steward know what you need. We tend to use them for items like ice, more towels, or extra pillows.

Sometimes, we like to **leave our steward a note** just to let him know we appreciate his hard work.

MAKE YOUR CABIN DOOR STAND OUT

It's surprisingly easy to walk by your cruise cabin door. We've done this hundreds of times. Every cabin door looks identical. If you're not paying attention (or had a couple "drinks of the day"), then it's **easy to miss** your room.

Any cabin **door decoration** will fix this. Whether it's a balloon, whiteboard, post-it note, or other. As long as something is on there, it'll be much easier to notice.

MAGNETIC HOOKS

Most people don't know that their cruise cabin **walls are metal**. And, as such, magnetic!

These super cheap <u>magnetic wall hooks</u> are great for organization.

They're great for holding our cruise card lanyards. We'll attach one near the door so we never forget to take it off and on as we come in and out.

It's also great for hats, bathing suits, jewelry and other lightweight items that otherwise clutter up flat areas.

BRIBE… ERR APPRECIATE YOUR CABIN STEWARD

A small token of appreciation goes a long way with your cabin steward. They work extremely hard and rarely receive **something "extra."**

This could be almost anything. As long as it shows some consideration, they'll appreciate it. They already offer great service, but will go even more "above and beyond" in this case.

We always bring a set of these **Cruise Staff Thank You Cards**. Sometimes we'll include a few bucks in there and other times just a nice note. Either way, the reaction is always heartwarming!

TRAVEL FAN

Cruise cabins aren't like a hotel, where you're able to adjust your personal thermostat. You'll likely be at the mercy of a central cooling unit, which you can't control.

As such, chances are you'll either be too hot or too cold. For those that are too cold, you can add layers. For those **too warm**, well, you can only shed so many until you're naked on top of your covers.

We bring a **small, travel fan**. In addition to keeping us cool, it also provides a nice white noise to drown out the ambient sounds.

AVOID A STUFFY CABIN

Cabins are small and can get a little...um, **"un-fresh"** after a few days of beach, pool, and other activities. Particularly, cabins without a balcony.

We like to bring an **air freshener** and some **Febreze** with us for a light misting once a day or so. It'll really help keep away those musty odors.

TAME THE POOP DECK

We don't particularly enjoy "potty talk," but this is an important cruise hack. As the saying goes, "everyone poops"... and this is particularly true on cruise ships. The difference here is that you're confined to a 200 square-foot area surrounding the toilet.

The person who invented **Poo Pourri** must have been a cruiser. This brilliant company has the slogan, "spritz the bowl before-you-go and no one else will ever know!"

CHOOSE YOUR BALCONY WISELY

If you're planning to get a balcony, your experience could vary significantly based on **the side of the ship** you choose.

Look at your itinerary closely and choose either **starboard or port side** based on the direction of the ship.

If your path is a clockwise circle, book a balcony cabin on the left-hand (port) side. If counter-clockwise, get a cabin on the starboard (right) side. That way, you'll have a view of the coast as you're coming and going.

DRY ERASE BOARD

This can be a really fun cruise accessory to add to your **cabin door**. Particularly if you're cruising with a group of friends or family.

It's always a fun surprise to come back to your cabin and have a note from someone you know… or someone that you don't!

With communication being so difficult on cruise ships, this is a great tool. If you're headed to the casino, pool, show, dinner or wherever, you can **let any visitors know**. Simply write it on your dry erase board and everyone stopping by will know where to find you.

And, they're under $5 on Amazon!

PUT SUITCASES UNDER YOUR BED

While this seems so obvious, we're always surprised when friends and family put suitcases in their closet. This takes up half of their space! And clothing items must be over these bags.

The beds are high enough to **fit suitcases underneath**.

Additionally, we like to throw worn clothes in them as we go about our week. It keeps them out of the way. But, I'd give those soiled clothes a quick Febreze spray first!

USE THE GYM SHOWER

Have you every felt cramped in a cruise shower? If not, it's likely that you haven't taken a cruise shower.

They're tiny! And there's barely enough space outside of the shower to get ready. There's definitely not enough room for two people!

A simple solution - use the **spa / fitness gym**. They typically have full size bathrooms and showers with plenty of room to get ready. And very few people take advantage of these.

When choosing your cabin, make sure to get one close enough to the fitness area to make this convenient for you.

CHAPTER 6

YOUNG KIDS ON A CRUISE

A cruise makes for an amazing vacation for the whole family. If you're traveling with little ones, know the tricks and trips to making everyone happy and comfortable.

CHILD PROOF WITH TAPE

If you're worried about toddlers bumping their little heads, bring a **roll of tape** to secure corners. You can use washcloths and other material to soften those edges.

It also comes in handy to **keep drawers shut** from those little explorers.

YOUNG KIDS ON A CRUISE

PICK A CABIN "UP AND BACK"

Typically, kids are most attracted to the features of a cruise ship located at the **top, rear (aft)** of the ship. These activities include mini-golf, pools, sporting activities, buffet, and more.

You'll likely be frequenting these areas and should consider booking a cabin nearby to avoid long treks.

EQUIP YOUR CHILD WITH A WATCH

Have your kids wear a watch. Finding the time on a ship is surprisingly difficult. There are **very few clocks** around to easily tell what time it is.

You'll likely be telling your kids, "meet me here at whatever O'clock."

To make it easier for them (and to eliminate excuses), have them **wear a watch!**

CRUISE LINES HAVE IT

Don't be shy to ask your room steward for whatever you'll need to take care of your little ones! Cruise lines are becoming much more aware of your **parenting necessities** and they're preparing for your requests. Here are a few items that are asked for more frequently than you'd expect:

- Pack & Plays / Cribs
- Pureed food
- Baby food

KEEP KIDS FROM SPENDING TOO MUCH

You have the option to enable or disable purchases on your child's ship card. We won't recommend one way or the other. But, we would like to remind you of the **many temptations** for kids on the ship. There's the arcade, shops, candy stores, and more where the cruise line makes it a little too easy to spend money.

SHIP TO DISNEY

For baby supplies, here's a hack that most don't know.

You can actually **ship baby essentials to Disney** up to two weeks ahead of time. They'll deliver these items to your cabin so you can free up some packing space.

Get in touch with the cruise line to find out where to ship based on departure port.

LANYARDS ARE A MUST

Kids love to lose things. Make it tricky for them with lanyards.

We never cruise without bringing **lanyards with ID holders**. Kiddos particularly love these and they make for great souvenirs from your vacation. They'll have a blast picking between the many styles available on Amazon.

These are our favorite **cruise card lanyards**.

YOUNG KIDS ON A CRUISE

VIP KIDDIE SERVICE

If sailing Disney, on first arriving tell your host the you'd like to participate in the "**Dine and Play**" plan.

It's for kids ages 3 to 12 and is during the second dinner seating.

Your little ones will get rushed-service and a surprise visit from staff. Best of all, this allows parents to enjoy some quality **alone time**!

YOUNG KIDS ON A CRUISE

PACKING SWIMSUITS ON DAY ONE

Once you get on the ship, the kids will likely B-line it to the pools. Make sure to **pack their swimsuits** in your carry-on bag. Otherwise, you could be waiting until evening to have these available (once the staff drops off your bags).

CHAPTER 7

ON-BOARD MONEY SAVING TIPS

It's fairly easy to score a good deal on a cruise. It takes more discipline to save money while on-board. The ship is designed to sell. Know the hacks to avoid a huge bill.

AIRPLANE MODE = SAFE MODE

Call your cell service provider. Tell them exactly where you're going and ask them where your network extends.

It's likely that you'll leave your network area in the trip.

To **assure no outrageous fees**, put your device in "Airplane Mode."

With Airplane Mode on, you're **still able to connect to WiFi**. So, for example, if you leave the ship at port. You can still connect to outside networks (like Starbucks or a local library). There you can make VOIP calls or send messages over iMessage or another internet texting service.

Taking your device out of airplane mode, however, can immediately start racking up your costs without you knowing it. As soon as the ship departs, go into Airplane Mode!

FREE DANCE LESSONS

Often, cruise ships will host dancing **lessons for free**.

If you've always wanted to take dance lessons, this is a great opportunity to test the waters, so to say. Check your daily planner where these will be listed.

THE LIBRARY IS YOUR FRIEND

Every cruise ship we've sailed has a Library.

Rather than spending money and lugging around heavy reading material, use the free resources of **your on-board library**. In addition to books, they often have magazines, games and more!

MAKE MONEY WHILE CRUISING

This might be one of the most underrated cruise hacks ever.

Don't let your empty home go to waste while you're out, **consider renting it on AirBnB**. In many locations, you can make more than it actually cost to cruise.

This is our favorite post showing **AirBnB rental rates vs Cruise Costs**. It breaks it down by city so you can see exactly how much your house will bring in vs average cruise cost based on your nearest departure port.

SPECIALTY DINE ON NIGHT ONE

Check to see if your cruise line offers a deal in their specialty dining restaurants on night one.

Often, you'll find a discounted per-person rate or an incentive, like a free bottle of wine. If you're planning to do a specialty dining night, **eating out on the first evening** could save some cash.

MOCHA COFFEE CHEAT

Most items on cruise ships are free, except **specialty coffees**.

Avoid this extra cost and enjoy your mocha coffee without pulling out that cruise card.

At the buffet, you'll find packets of **cocoa mix** along with creamers. Add those to your coffee and you'll feel like you just robbed a Starbucks.

DOWNLOAD THE SHIP'S MOBILE APP IN ADVANCE

Your cruise line likely has a free mobile app to use on-board offering helpful features like the ability to check your bill, see activities, restaurant menus, and more.

But, you'll want to make sure to **download this BEFORE you set sail**, or it'll cost you!

While still on the mainland, use these links to download your cruise line's mobile app.

Carnival	Carnival HUB (iOS)	Carnival HUB (Android)
Royal Caribbean	Royal Caribbean (iOS)	Royal Caribbean (Android)
Norwegian	NCL iConcierge (iOS)	NCL iConcierge (Android)
Celebrity	Celebrity Cruises (iOS)	Celebrity Cruises (Android)
Princess	Download on board (iOS)	Download on board(Android)
Disney	Disney Navigator (iOS)	Disney Navigator (Android)

LIBERTY, FREEDOM & INDEPENDENCE OF THE SEAS BUTT BONUS

This is probably the funniest cruise hack that we know.

If you're sailing one of these three ships, consider getting **cabin 6305**.

- Liberty of the Seas
- Freedom of the Seas
- Independence of the Seas

Your rear window overlooks two cows' butts.

As a consolation, Royal Caribbean will give you **free Ben & Jerry's** every day as well as access to the **special concierge lounge** (reserved for suite passengers).

SAVE SHOPPING UNTIL THE END

Most ships have a shopping area. If you're looking to save, **wait until the last couple days** of the sailing. Items tend to go on sale at that point.

SPA DAY

If you're planning a day at the Spa, save some money by **visiting during a port** stop. On every ship we've sailed, the cruise line offers a good discount while the ship is at port.

AVOID ATM FEES

ATM's on cruise ships **have huge fees**. On our last ship, the combined fees were over $15.

To avoid these completely, go to the casino. You can use your card to extract cash for little or no cost.

EXTRACT ON-BOARD CREDITS

If you don't use your on-board credits, **they'll go to waste**. You obviously don't want this to happen.

You can easily convert this on-board credit to cash. Use your sail card to deposit money into your casino's nearest slot machine.

Don't gamble this away - simply pull it out as a voucher and have the **purser turn it into cash**.

CHAPTER 8

WIFI SECRETS

Cruise ships are still operating in the stone ages when it comes to Wifi. Rates are absurd and connection poor! Use these tips to avoid online frustration and a large bill.

WIFI SECRETS

PURCHASE WIFI IN ADVANCE

We like to go offline while on-board, but understand that not everyone can do that for certain reasons.

If you're planning to connect while at sea, **purchase your package beforehand**. You'll often save by doing this.

GET PUSHY

Don't assume you have to pay for service to get any access to the internet. We've heard from a few people that **push notifications can slip through** even if you have no paid plan.

Before you ship off, turn your device to "Airplane Mode" and then **connect to the cruise ship's "Intranet."** It should be obvious from the network name what that is (i.e. "Carnival Dream Guest Wifi"). Once you connect, you're all set. You may get notices (iMessage, FB Messenger, etc) that pop up unfiltered by the cruise ship.

Note: you won't be able to respond to any of these unless you pay for access to the network.

KEEP IT UNDER 30

Often we need to connect for a specific reason… to see if someone responded to an email, to check a score, send a quick message, etc. If you **keep it under 30 seconds**, you won't be charged on some ships.

Just log in, then do whatever is necessary (very quickly) and log out. Make it a game. This is true for Celebrity and other lines as well.

Combine this with our next hack to actually get some work done, for free!

COMPOSE FIRST SEND AFTER

Sometimes it's inevitable. We HAVE to do work while on-board. And most of the time, this consists of sending emails.

Here's a simple, yet very effective, way to minimize cost. **Compose all of those emails BEFORE getting online**. There's no reason to type out your communications while paying for each passing second. You'll likely know who you need to contact and for what reason in advance.

Put all emails together while offline, then **log in and fire those off**. If you combine this tactic with our previous hack, you may be able to get a decent amount of work done, completely free!

USE THE NETWORK WHEN OTHERS AREN'T

Cruise lines' progress regarding internet speeds is poor. While most offer Wifi, it's painfully slow. Particularly during peak times when many other passengers are using it.

If using the network when it's crowded, it could take more than twice as long to get anything done. That will cost twice as much. To avoid paying extra, **use the Internet when others aren't**. Dinner time, late night, early morning, and during show times are good examples when usage will be minimal.

USE WIFI NEAR THE SOURCE

Typically, network routers are positioned near your **cruise ship's Internet Lab**. The service will be much stronger here than other areas throughout the ship.

Visit the lab when you see that it's empty. The network should be faster when you have exclusive use.

CALL YOUR PROVIDER

You may be surprised at the coverage your carrier provides. **Call customer service** and figure out exactly where your network extends.

On our last cruise, we were delighted to learn that the Caribbean was included in our service. Having network access at your cruise port can be incredibly helpful. And, it might be a free option. **Just check!**

WIFI SECRETS

PAY FOR WHAT YOU GET

On our last sailing, the Internet was practically unusable. We let the Desk Manager know how poor it was, and was **fully refunded**. Like with most services on your cruise, if not up to practical standards, you should let your passenger services desk know and they'll typically be willing to help.

WIFI SECRETS

ASK CREW MEMBERS

The crew knows all! Including where and how to access the Internet. They'll be very familiar with the ship and ports. **Ask them** where the best internet service is both on-board and off. One of your crew members should be happy to share the secret hotspots.

DRINKING ON A BUDGET

On a few cruises, we partied a little too much. Our final bill dwarfed the cost of the cruise.
It's a Titanic feeling that we'll help you avoid.

BUY IN BULK

If you're buying beers for a group, or plan to have a few, see if a **"bucket deal"** is available. If so, you'll save at least a buck per beer. And, you won't have to get up each time you're done. The ice-filled bucket can sit there next to you so you only have to move to use the bathroom.

You'll also find **wine packages** available. You can purchase multiple bottles for the week and save a few bucks vs buying them individually.

PRE-ORDER BOOZE

Some ships will let you **pre-purchase liquor** and will have it waiting for you in your room.

We've heard of bottles of whiskey going for under $40 on Holland America.

Check with your cruise line to see if you can pre-purchase bottles of booze.

CHOOSE A WINE BOTTLE VS GLASS

If you'll be having wine on multiple nights, a **bottle will be significantly cheaper** than ordering four separate glasses.

The dining staff will be happy to re-cork your bottle at the end of dinner and bring it back later in the week (or later that night).

PARTY WHILE AT PORT

If you're in the mood to have a few drinks, just know that it'll cost way less while at port when compared to ship prices.

Typically a beer will cost around $5 on the ship. At many ports, you can find a great locally brewed beer **for around $1**!

Just don't get too excited or you'll end up on YouTube as a "pier runner."

HAPPY HOUR SAVINGS

While it's rarely advertised, most ships have **happy hours** at varying bars throughout the ship.

Ask your customer service desk or look for this info posted around the bar.

You'll often find a "**drink of the day**" and discounts up to $5 on other beverages.
This can really add up over the course of a cruise! Or, you can have more for the same price if you'd rather.

BYOB

Most cruise lines allow you to **bring your own wine**. Typically a 750ml bottle. This is a great chance to save money. A $20 bottle from BevMo might cost $80 on the ship.

You can also then enjoy it from your balcony.

Make sure to check your specific cruise line's rules.

SMUGGLE LIKE A PIRATE

We **don't condone** smuggling alcohol onto the ship.

While the penalty is merely confiscation, it's still embarrassing and your fellow passengers may be paying for your cheating ways in the form of premium prices.

That said, we know that many will still try. Here are the **most common** (and most hilarious) ways that we've heard.

- Rum Runner Plastic Bladders
- Shampbooze (fake shampoo bottles)
- Fake Sunscreen Flasks (not joking)
- Sippin Scarf (our favorite - what?!)

WAIT ON THAT BEER

While still in the immediate vicinity of some ports, you'll be **charged tax** on drinks. That tax disappears as soon as you get far enough away from port.

This tax is also applied to your "all you can drink" package. It'll still cost you while nearby port.

Ask your bartender if there's a tax and **when it's lifted** to avoid a few extra dollars in charges.

TOAST TO THE CAPTAIN

Most cruises have a "Captain's Party" on Night One of your sailing.

The staff will hand out champagne and sometimes other drink options. This is a great start to the first evening a good way to get a free couple drinks.

FREE LIQUOR TASTINGS

Your ship will have a store to purchase alcohol. Unfortunately, they won't give you the bottle right then and there, but will wait until the end of your cruise.

But, fortunately, they will have **one or two free liquor tastings** during the week. Stop by to try some new fermented treats and to get a free buzz on.

STOP AT THE ART AUCTION

The more cruisers drink, the more they're likely to spend on expensive art. The cruise line knows this, so will often serve **free champagne at their art auctions**.

Note, you'll need to have some discipline to make this work. Getting a free drink won't help your budget if you end up with a new $5k mural for your mantle.

CHAPTER 10

DINING ON BOARD

Cruising and dining go together like steak and mashed potatoes. Here are a few extra hints to get even more great food, dining options, and excellent service.

CRUISE DINING

YOUR OPTIONS ARE LIMITLESS

Don't think about your cruise dining service like you would a restaurant. You're **not paying "a la carte"**. And you're not limited to what you see on the menu.

Feel free to order multiple appetizers or multiple entrees. You can even order appetizers as your entree, if you'd like. Or, ask for something from a previous night or even from the kids' menu. Whatever your heart (and appetite) desire **is a possibility** in your cruise ship's dining room.

CRUISE DINING

EXPAND YOUR BREAKFAST REACH

Most cruisers assume the buffet is the only place to get breakfast.

Often, **ships offer alternative options** in other cafes, bars, and even specialty dining restaurants. And, all are complimentary.

You'll likely avoid crowds by branching out as well.

CRUISE DINING

ASK FOR ALL MENUS

Visit your front desk and ask to see the **week's prepared menus** for the main dining room. All meals are planned for the entire week.

This will allow you to plan accordingly if you're thinking about skipping the main dining room one night. That way, you won't miss your favorite meal!

CRUISE DINING

COFFEE SHOPS

Typically, there are on-board cafes available on your ship. They serve high-end coffees for an extra cost.

But, the **snacks** they offer at these venues are **at NO cost**. You'll find a nice variety of bites that you won't see elsewhere on the ship.

CRUISE DINING

GET THE BEST TABLE

Snag a VIP table. On Day 1 of your sailing, visit your maître d'
before dining service starts. Be extra nice to him and simply request
a good table. He'll probably ask for your card or info and you're likely
to get hooked up with a VIP spot.

CRUISE DINING

AVOID BUFFET LUNCH ON DAY ONE

As soon as everyone gets on the ship, most rush straight to the buffet. People are hungry after their travels and they don't know of other dining options.

Do some research beforehand to **find alternative lunch spots**. They'll be empty on embarkation day and you'll avoid the chaos.

CRUISE DINING

REQUEST YOUR FAVORITE AGAIN

If you've had something that was amazing… so amazing, that you have to **have it again**, simply ask your dining staff. They'll often be happy to save some or prepare it again later in the week. This isn't a guarantee, but worth the try.

CRUISE DINING

CHOOSE YOUR SPECIALTY DINING NIGHT

We advise trying a specialty dining option for at least one night.

How do you know which night to choose? **Pick your favorite meal beforehand!** The specialty dining venues will publicly post the current day's menu. But, the whole week is planned. Ask to see the full lineup and choose your favorite dish and therefore your ideal night.

CRUISE DINING

TREAT YOURSELF TO ROOM SERVICE

Room service on a cruise isn't like room service in a hotel. Often it's free or a minimal charge.

Make sure to **check the room service details** in your cabin info or call and ask guest services. Some will have different fees based on the time of day.

CRUISE DINING

DOUBLE ENTREE HACK

Often, we can't decide between two delicious-looking entrees on the main menu. We could order both, but don't want that much food in front of us at once.

The hack… order the entree's main dish **as an appetizer**. You can get it without the frills (rice, potato, etc) so it's just the main event as an appetizer. This works great with vegetarian entrees too!

CRUISE DINING

GET DIETARY RESTRICTIONS RECORDED EARLY

Do you have particular **dietary restrictions**? Vegan, lactose intolerance, allergies? Let the cruise line know before you sail. They'll make sure to be prepared.

When you get to the dining room on Day 1, show up early and make sure to **introduce yourself** and your needs. Remind your staff on Night 2 just to be sure they associate your face with your needs. The staff is usually very good with memorizing faces.

CRUISE DINING

MAKE TABLE CHANGES EARLY

Make sure to let your dining staff know on night 1 **if you're not happy** with your seating arrangement.

If you're allocated a seating time or table and you're not happy with what you are given, **request changes** as soon into your trip as possible. If you're celebrating a special occasion and don't want to be seated with others, you can put this request in then too.

SWEET TREATS

If you're looking for a sweet treat, the buffet isn't your only option. While the cafes charge for specialty coffee, they typically have great **little sweets for free**. And you'll avoid the crowds.

FREE CANDY

We all get a sweet tooth and it tends to happen more often on a cruise.

If you're a candy fan like us, then this is a great hack. Don't spend $5 for a bag of sweets at the shop. Instead, **go to the ice cream stand**. Check out the toppings and find your favorite (M&M's, Oreos, Gummy Bears, etc). Ask the server for a cup and she'll be happy to hand that over.

CHAPTER 11

PORT TIPS

You have a very limited time while on shore. You'll typically get to port early in the morning and ship off around dusk. Make the most of that short time with these hacks.

LISTEN TO SOME LOCAL TUNES

Get a feel for the local culture by bringing a **portable radio**. At port, you'll actually be able to get a surprising number of radio stations.

Listen to the **local broadcast** to start your day on your balcony, or bring your radio to shore to take on your adventure.

This is our favorite portable radio.

FOLLOW THE STAFF FOR WIFI

One of the best ways to get free internet is to **follow the staff**. They'll swarm off the ship to get onto their laptops and devices.

They know exactly where to go for free wifi. Follow or ask them where you can do the same.

GO FURTHER FOR BETTER INTERNET

For free and comfortable internet access, look for a **Starbucks or a public library**. Both should offer what you need as well as a cozy setting.

If neither are available, an internet cafe might be the only option. To save money at one of these, venture further away from the ship. The closest options will be the most expensive.

PACK A LUNCH

At most U.S. and some Caribbean ports, you're allowed to **take food off of the ship**.

You can save a bundle by preparing a snack to take along to shore. A couple sandwiches and some fruit should hold you over until you get back.

Ports tend to overprice food and this is a great way to save.

PORT INFO BOOK

These aren't handed out to everyone. They're usually given to those that attend the **port lecture**. Included in this material are helpful maps, tips, coupons and more. They can save a lot of money and heartache.

If you don't feel like going to the port lecture, simply **ask guest relations for one of these helpful books**, and they should be happy to accommodate.

PORT TIPS

NEGOTIATING IS WORTH A TRY

When purchasing goods, don't be afraid to **negotiate the price**. If an item is $60, for example, offer $40. It might not work, but the worst that can happen is you're denied. Often, you'll save money just by asking.

DON'T USE DEBIT CARDS

We've heard horror stories of **fraudulent charges** from individuals who used a debit card for purchases.

To avoid this, use a credit card or cash. If fake charges appear on your card, you can always reach out to your provider to dispute these.

PORT TIPS

BRING WATER & STAY HYDRATED

You're going to **need water** during your active day ashore. Local vendors know this and tend to overcharge for H20.

To prepare, bring a water container with you on your cruise. You can fill it up on the ship and take it with you to port. Get a quality insulated one of good size, and it'll **keep cold and quench your thirst** for the entire day. As an added bonus, it's more environmentally friendly.

This brand, from Travel Kuppe, is insulated and comes in various sizes. We have the big 32 ounce version and it works perfectly.

CHAPTER 12

SHORE EXCURSIONS TIPS

Most cruisers take part in an "excursion" when getting to port. This can vary from jet skiing to snorkeling to a museum. Get the experience at the best price with these tips.

BOOK EXCURSIONS IN ADVANCE

Don't wait until the last minute to book your shore excursion. There are two main reasons for taking care of this in advance.

1. Often, the more **popular trips will sell out**: lock in your ideal shore tour in the months before your cruise so that it doesn't sell out.
2. **Don't wait in line** when you can be relaxing: it's your vacation. You won't want to be waiting in lines and dealing with logistics.

Whether you book with the cruise line or a third-party, lock in your activity before your sail date.

ASK THE STAFF

Staff members have probably been to your ports many times. As such, they should be familiar with the best activities to do while in port.

Ask various staff members what they consider the best option on shore. Some will give you the most popular activity (what they think you want to hear), while others might give you some hidden gems.

USING A 3ʳᵈ PARTY VS THE CRUISE LINE

You have **three main options** when booking port excursions. Your "best" option will vary based on your priorities. Here's our breakdown of each option.

- **Use the Cruise Line to book**: the up-side here is the convenience factor. You'll have the **easiest time** booking and coordinating your trip when using the line itself. The downside is you'll spend a bit more and your options may be limited.

- **Use a Major Third-Party to book**: you can find additional options by looking outside of the cruise lines. But, we only advise this if using a reputable provider. The largest out there is <u>Viator</u>. Two of our other favorites include <u>Shore Excursions Group</u> and <u>Shorefox</u>. You can absolutely trust all three of these groups. The cruise lines will tell you that it's risky to use these groups, but that is 100% false. All three will assure you get back to your ship and uses the same providers as the cruise line. You'll likely be on the same trip as others, but at a fraction of the price. Here's a great hack to easily search all three of these providers. Use this new site, <u>Gangwaze.com</u> - they pull all excursions from these three providers into one place so you don't need to visit multiple web sites!

- **Go direct**: if you're comfortable with risk, you can use reach out directly to the provider or just approach an excursion company while at port. The downsides are obvious here. You could miss your ship, get ripped off, or worse. **We don't recommend this option**.

SOUVENIRS

If you're planning to purchase souvenirs before you go home, look for a **shopping excursion**. You can likely get all the gifts and souvenirs in one swoop. And, they should be way less expensive than trying to purchase something on the ship.

PORT TIME VS SHIP TIME

This can get confusing. There's "**ship time**" and there's "**port time**." Most of the time, they're the same. But not *all* the time.

Triple check which one your ship is using to determine your required time back on board. Once you're sure, set your device to that proper time, add an alert for at least an hour before your return time. That should give you enough time to get back to ship.

THINK OUTSIDE THE BOX

One great option that most don't know about - get a **Resort Day Pass**!

If you want some structure to your day, but would rather relax than get active, then this is a great option.

At many ports, you can pay to use a **resort's many amenities and attractions**. Often, they'll include perks like free drinks, water sports, hammocks, and much more. You'll also have the option to go "All Inclusive" for a reasonable price. You can check out your **Resort for a Day Options here**.

START FAR AND END CLOSE

If you're like us, you like to explore as much of the island as possible.

We advise that you start exploring the farthest area from port to start and **work your way back** to the ship. That way, you're much less likely to miss the ship's departure. You never know what can go wrong. If there's a hiccup or time gets away from you, you'll want to be close to port.

BREAKFAST IN BED TO SAVE TIME

Don't risk missing your excursion. The buffet will be packed on port arrival days. Everyone is trying to get a bite before leaving the ship. Don't battle the crowds.

The night before you port, **order room service** to arrive at your door when you're waking up.

CHAPTER 13

HEALTH AND WEIGHT TIPS

Don't worry, we're not going to tell you that you can't indulge. You're on vacation and there's endless options for delicious food. Use these tips to feel your best!

ONLY TAKE THE STAIRS

This is a GREAT way to get a workout without actually going to the gym, running, or committing to a prolonged period of activity.

Throughout your sailing, you'll need to travel from deck to deck to get to different venues. Most people take the elevator. **Taking the stairs is so much better**. In addition to getting your exercise, you're saving time and the headache of cramming into a confined space with strangers.

We wore our fitbit on our last cruise and were taking close to 12,000 steps per day, with about 10% of those being stairs. We've estimated an **extra 600 calories** burned per day by opting for the stairs. Come dinner time, you'll really have earned that second dessert!

REMOVE THE BLAH FOOD

Like restaurants, cruise dining rooms operate strategically. They know you'll eat bread if it's in front of you. The bread that costs them a penny will fill your appetite which would otherwise be satisfied by a filet costing the cruise line $5.

It's not just about getting the most bang for your bite. Bread is empty carbs. Little nutrients or protein… just empty weight gain.

For these reasons, ask your server to **only serve bread with your entree**. That way you're not denying yourself the indulgence, but you'll be much less tempted to go for the bread when you have the main event in front of you.

DON'T GET FRUITY

When getting cocktails, the brighter they are, the worse they are for you (typically). While very enticing, those **"umbrella drinks"** are loaded with sugar. Not only are they terrible for your health, but you're likely to wake up with a hangover due to the extra sugar!

Stick with wine, light beer, or mixers with no sugar (like club soda).

HEARTS ON FIRE

The week of wine and food might catch up to you in the form of heartburn. Prepare for this by packing your favorite **antacid**. These heartburn medicines tend to be heavily marked up in the ship's general store.

DRY SKIN HACK

You might notice your skin drying out from the salt water, sun, and extra activity. If you're getting a little extra ashy on your elbows and knees, use a lemon! **Rubbing a lemon** on dry spots of your skin will almost instantly relieve symptoms. Your dining staff will be happy to oblige your fruit request.

HYDRATE LIKE A CAMEL

This is one of the most effective (yet so simple) ideas to stay healthy on your cruise… **stay hydrated**!

But, it's not easy unless you follow this hack. Bring along a **large, travel water container** with you. It's very difficult to get enough water with the small cups that they offer. Bring a 24 ounce (or larger) travel container and suck it down at least twice per day (we recommend 4 times). This is <u>what we use on every sailing</u>.

You'll stay less hungry, less hung over, and less prone to illness!

BECOME A TEMPORARY GERMAPHOBE

We've all heard the nightmare cruise stories. The LAST thing you want is to catch **"the bug"** and wind up quarantined to your cabin for the remainder of your cruise.

You get sick by ingesting germs after coming into contact with these. There are **two great ways** to avoid this.

1. Don't stick your hands in your mouth.
2. Constantly wash and use the ship's antibacterial foam or gel.

USE THE SHIP'S OUTSIDE AMENITIES

Cruise ships have many amenities that allow you to get active. These offer a great (and fun) way to burn some extra calories.

Plan at least **one physical activity per day**, even if that's a long walk around the ship. If you'd like to get a little sweaty, try some basketball, ping pong, swimming, rock climbing, etc.

GIVE STAFF A HEADS UP

For ANY medical condition that you feel is important, make sure to **inform the cruise line** very soon after booking.

They'll take the necessary steps to assure that your issue is addressed. Whether you require an extension cord for a CPAP machine or hyper-allergenic pillow covers or any other unusual request... do not wait until last minute to talk to the cruise line or your agent!

GET A GRIP

The surrounding outer ship area can get slippery at times.

Bring a pair of comfortable and, preferably, **rubber-soled shoes or sandals**. You'll be doing a lot of walking so you want to be sure to stay comfortable and slip-free.

DON'T BE "THAT GUY"

On every cruise we've sailed, there's at least one "that guy."

He's so excited to be in the sun, that he relishes every minute of the glorious rays. The next day, he's miserable in the corner with towels draped over him.

Sometimes, it's even more serious (sun poisoning is a real thing). Make sure you ease into the hopefully great weather. Particularly on Day 1, **lather up and wear a hat**! On a cruise ship, the ray's reflections on the ship and water can be misleading. And time tends to fly by as well. Don't be "that guy!"

GET AROUND AT PORT

At almost every cruise port, you'll find opportunities to get active through **organized excursions**. These range from hiking, to horseback riding, to jet-skiing to snorkeling. If looking to get a workout, search Gangwaze.com for excursions and use the filter "active" or even "extreme" to find the most physical tours.

If these options don't exist (at privately owned ports for example) then take a long walk to explore.

ON-BOARD PRACTICAL HACKS

You'll be among thousands of cruisers with limited knowledge. With these on-board hacks, you'll be one step ahead in getting around the ship most efficiently.

BE WHERE THEY AREN'T

One of the biggest complaints about a cruise is the crowd size. People get frustrated because they're herded around with the masses.

We do the opposite. When everyone is still asleep, we're walking around the pool. While others are in the main dining room, we're using the rock climbing wall or Flowrider. When cruisers head to port, we'll stick around and enjoy the amenities we've been waiting to use.

RESEARCH IS THE KEY

Cruise ships are huge! You don't want to go into your sailing completely blind. Before we knew of this hack, we'd always feel like we missed out after our cruise was over. We'd end the week having never seen half of the ship's amenities.

Now, we know better. In the months before our vacation, we'll **look over every inch of the ship and its features**. We'll note all of the features that we want to see during the week. That way, there's no missing out.

The best way to easily view a ship's **deck maps and amenities** is using our favorite cruise app, Ship Mate.

Download **Ship Mate for iOS** and **Ship Mate for Android** free!

FIND YOUR ZEN SPOT

On every ship, there are nooks and crannies that 99% of passengers don't know about. This might be the library, card room, or obscure sitting space somewhere. When the crowd is getting overwhelming, **return to your zen spot** for some solace. We'll return to ours on a daily basis for an hour for some silence and a good book.

USE THE CHAT APP

Most ships now offer an internal communications tool on the ship, via their **mobile app**. We neglect how often we text throughout the day until it's no longer an option.

To solve for this issue, most cruise lines offer a mobile app **specifically for texting**. For a relatively small fee (less than $10), you'll be able to text all other members with the app. This can save a great deal of time otherwise spent scouring the ship for your friends and family.

We provide all download links to major cruise apps in our other hack here.

RAIN IS YOUR VIP PASS

It always amazes us that people leave the pool area when it rains... like getting wet is unacceptable all of a sudden. **When it rains**, we view this as the best opportunity to use the hot tubs and water slides. You'll avoid big lines and crowds this way. And, you were going to get wet anyway, so who cares about a little rain?

DOWNLOAD ENTERTAINMENT

Whether it's a podcast, audio book, or good music, you'll want to have it on your ship. There's nothing better than finding a beach chair and good drink and some quality entertainment. Make sure to **download your entertainment of choice in advance** so it's stored on your device. You won't be able to access it otherwise, or it'll cost you an arm and a leg.

Download at least 20 hours of audio books, music or podcast to keep you going through the cruise.

DAILY PLANNER DAILY PICTURE

When you wake up, you'll find your Daily Planner slipped under your cruise cabin door. **Take a picture** with your smart phone right away.

This **accomplishes two things**. The more obvious of the two - it makes it easy to refer to the planner throughout the day. You don't worry about folding it up, drying it off, losing it, etc. You simply whip out your phone and it's there.

Here's the less obvious advantage to taking this picture. If you consistently snap a pic each morning, it helps you to **easily sort your phone's pictures** that you take throughout the week. You'll compartmentalize each set of images by day. Your planner pic will let you know what day of the week and which port you're visiting!

GET THE GOOD SEATS

Use this hack to get the best seats in the theater.

In most ships, there will be four entrances to the main event theater: upper right, upper left, lower right, & lower left. You'll want to use one specific entrance for the best seats. Find the entrance in front of **the non-pass-through corridor**.

Typically this is the least accessed and you'll find the **most empty seats** right there inside.

GET YOUR BILL EARLY

On the final morning there will be a **huge line** of individuals disputing transactions on their final bill. That's not where you want to be during your final moments on the ship.

Instead, ask for a printout on **the night before** you arrive back in port. Check through your charges and make sure to clear up any discrepancies at that point. You'll be very glad that you did!

KNOW YOUR BAGGAGE WEIGHT

If you're planning to purchase items while on your cruise, know how much leeway you have before you hit that 50 pound limit imposed by airlines.

Either bring a **small travel scale** with you or weigh it and leave the scale at home. You should be able to roughly estimate the weight of the items you purchase while at sea. As a reference, three t-shirts will be just over a pound.

If you're really worried and want to get a measurement, know that there's a scale that you can use **in the gym**. It'll be a pain to lug your bag up there, but it could save you some money.

SEA SICKNESS PREVENTION

Sea sickness can ruin your cruise. Once it sets in, it's very difficult to recover. The goal is to avoid any onset. Otherwise, you could be destined for a very long week.

SEA SICKNESS

CABIN PLACEMENT

If you're at all worried about getting sea-sick, make sure to follow this hack. Select your cabin on the **lower levels** of the ship and as **close to the middle** of the vessel as possible. That will assure the least amount of movement and lower your chances of getting sea sickness.

STAY COOL

Keep the air on in your cabin so it stays **as cool as possible**. The cold temperature will counteract motion sickness.

NATURAL REMEDY

Ginger has helped many people get over their proclivity to sea sickness. It has anti-nausea qualities that are particularly helpful to beating this ailment. It can be consumed in a number of ways. Here are a few **ginger options** to choose from.

- Ginger candies
- Ginger slices
- Ginger tea

GET BALANCED

Motion sickness occurs due to the rocking motion. There's only one spot on the ship that you can go to completely avoid moving with the ship… **the pool!**

Once floating, your inner ear fluids will become more stabilized, counteracting the motion sickness.

GREEN APPLE

We've heard of this tactic from a few people that swear by it. As soon as you feel any signs of motion sickness, try a **green apple**! They should be readily available in the buffet and have been known to result in almost immediate relief.

ORANGE WHIFF

The **smell of an orange** rind has been known to cause instant relief from sea sickness.

Just peel the orange, hold the rind up to your nose, and inhale.

CHAPTER 16

STAY SAFE

We want you to have a safe, happy and healthy cruise. Chances are that you'll have an amazing time. But, those chances are ever increased by using these hacks to stay safe.

DO NOT DISTURB

We like to keep the "**Do not disturb**" sign on our door when we're out and about. That makes it much less likely that someone will enter your cabin or hotel room.

ASSURE ITS SHUT

Cruise cabin doors have a tendency to **stay ajar** when passengers shut those. It's partly due to the air currents and also from the pressurization in the cabin areas. Never assume the door will shut completely when walking away. Always pull or push the cabin door completely shut **until it clicks**.

While cruise ships are relatively safe, it's inviting disaster to leave your cabin door open.

PHOTOCOPY YOUR DOCUMENTS

You'll have some important documents when traveling. Avoid a potential nightmare by taking **photocopies** of your most important pieces.

In the rare case that your documents getting lost or stolen, be prepared. With copies, you'll make it much easier on yourself in this unfortunate situation.

Here are some items we recommend photocopying.

- Visa
- Passport
- License
- Medicare card
- Cruise tickets
- Excursion vouchers
- Airline tickets

LOCK SLIDING DOORS

Always make sure your **sliding balcony door is properly locked**. It's very easy to gain access to cabins via the external connections between balconies. At port, it's also possible for contractors (painters, cleaners, etc) to get access to balconies. Make sure your sliding door is secure!

YOUR SAFE IS NOT SAFE

If you think your safe is safe, then tell your cabin steward that you're locked out of it. You'll watch as he **easily opens it** at your request. Personally, we don't trust a safe that can be opened by 1/3rd of the people on a ship.

USE A SAFE

While the cruise safe isn't the best option, we do recommend that you secure your goods. This is especially true while at port. We use **this travel safe** to lock up our valuables poolside, at port, and even in our cabin. We'll stick our phones, wallets, ship cards, and more in there while swimming in the pool or ocean. We'll also attach it to a fixture in our rooms and use that rather than the ship's assigned cabin safe.

SECURE YOUR GOODS AT PORT

When making your way around cruise ports, make sure to **secure your valuables**. Some ports have been known for pickpockets and other petty crimes. Carry your wallet in your front pockets. For purses, strap them so they're crossing the front of your body.

STOP ELECTRONIC THEFT

Electronic theft has quickly become one of the biggest financial threats to passengers. It can happen without the victim ever realizing it has occurred. The perpetrator can steal credit card and other info from an electronic gadget held within close proximity. To stop these attacks, we use an **RFID blocker**. It's a brilliant way to fight technology using technology.

Printed in Great Britain
by Amazon